Mountain Dharma
The Alchemy of Realization

Dudjom Rinpoche's *Richo*

Translated from the Tibetan
with an introduction
by
Keith Dowman

Published by Dzogchen Now! Books

www.radicaldzogchen.com

Copyright © Keith Dowman 2017

All rights reserved. No part of this book may be reproduced in any form or by any means, electronic or mechanical, including photography, recording, or by any information storage or retrieval system or technologies now known or later developed without permission in writing from the publisher.

ISBN-13 9 9781522763550

ISBN-10 1522763554

Printed in the U.S.A. Font set in Book Antigua

Cover design by James Moore.

Homage To Dudjom Rinpoche
Jigtral Yeshe Dorje

Dedicated to all sentient beings

Contents

Preface	7
Homage	13
The First Topic: Preparation: How to purify the mindstream by cutting clinging attachment and focusing the mind on the praxis.	26
The Second Topic: The Main Endeavour: How to engage directly in the practice after eradicating misconceptions and doubts about view, meditation and action.	32
The Third Topic: The Stream of Illuminated Existential Attainment: How to maintain the samayas, keep the vows and thus completely assimilate the karma of this lifetime to Dzogchen realization.	40
Glossary of Technical Terms	49

Preface

It should be noted that this text derived from a brilliant teaching given by my Guru-Lama, Dudjom Rinpoche Jigtral Yeshe Dorje (1904 – 1987), is from the traditional mould. In this state Dzogchen is inseparable from the Vajrayana of the Ngagyur Nyingma tradition. Here, Dzogchen is bound up with Tibetan Buddhism, which carries it and forms a basis for its practice. It was written for Tibetan yogis in Old Tibet where retirement to a hermitage was as easy as falling off a log and was expected of anyone – excluding tulkus – who had serious existential aspirations. As such, Tibetan cultural assumptions are implicit in it, assumptions that in general are at best irrelevant to Western Dzogchen aspirants and at worst lead away from the primary purpose – realization of the nature of mind. The text may be treated as an anthropological resource; but it only requires discriminating filtration to become a mine of useful precepts for radical Dzogchen practice. This is the 'heartblood' of a Dzogchen master.

Keith Dowman,
Tepoztlan,
Morelos, Mexico, 2017.

Preface to the 1999 Edition

In Tibet, mountain retreat in a cave or hermitage was the crucible of existential training. The great lamas of the tradition gained their realization in that way. In exile, the young tulkus pay lip service to that old tradition but most have relied on close association with their teachers and then closet themselves for extended periods in meditation centers. In our Western retreat centers we have copied this compromise between a hermitage and a monastery with varying results. Bearing in mind the difficulty of finding a mountain retreat in the West that approximates Dudjom Rinpoche's ideal, the text translated below urges Dzogchen aspirants to take a more extreme and committed path and to cultivate the qualities of renunciation in a secluded meditation cell.

In *Mountain Dharma: The Alchemy of Realization* Dudjom Rinpoche assumes that we need to cultivate the qualities of renunciation. We need to use our aspiration to abandon our inherited social and political system and its sticky imperatives and we need to remove ourselves from the proximate causes of sensory attachment. We leave our homeland, first of all, and leave behind a large part of our mental baggage and let another large part atrophy from lack of attention. When the time is ripe we meet a teacher and obtain initiation, authorization and oral instruction. Then we find a secluded hermitage in which to ripen our minds.

Certainly, there is no need to take this literal ascetic approach if we can find a cave in the mind rather than on the mountaintop. There is no need to move out of the urban environment if we are based in a space of inner detachment. There is no need to avoid sex and war if our Dzogchen view and meditation is complete and perfectly compassionate. The Dzogchen method and schedule supports this view, and meditation practiced in the city and the urban yogi are the putative results. The difficulties of this path, however, are evident to anyone who has lived it. We have been educated and conditioned to exist in the cultural mainstream and it is so easy to be pulled out of our cave of renunciation by the needs of survival and the intensity of the sensual and intellectual stimuli so readily available.

To assist us to remain in that inner cave there is nothing like a bit of celibacy, for instance, at least in the initial phase of renunciation, to get our sexual needs into perspective and keep our sexual fluids racing. A natural fast not only cleanses the stomach but it takes the obsession out of our gluttony. A period of simple happy living in country seclusion reduces the demands of consumerist city dwelling and its moneymaking imperatives. Make space between the mind and its objects of attachment and the sticky adhesive that creates confusion and delusion is dissolved, and clarity resumes. The renunciate mind puts space between samsara and ourselves and allows the superior aspiration for nirvana to click in.

Yes, of course, samsara is nirvana, but that old saw is more often used as an excuse for self-indulgence and distraction than the basis of the existential Dzogchen view. And, yes, the Dzogchen view, which is the foundation of all Dzogchen meditation, is inalienable and inescapable and can never be compromised. But the very act of reading this text, in many cases, indicates backsliding in meditation practice and implies a need for the renunciate view that may re-establish motivation for it. Always intrinsically based in the Dzogchen view and meditation, any means whatsoever may be utilized to regain full recognition of it. The renunciate mindset is a very valuable and effective skillful means.

In the short work below, in which he gives practical personalized advice to the Dzogchen aspirant, Dudjom Rinpoche assumes that his disciples have been born and bred in a traditional society that supports awareness-aspiration. He elucidates the traditional Nyingtik method that begins at the beginning and continues through the middle to the end. Renunciation and mountain retreat are ideals that perhaps only very fortunate Westerners can pursue. But regardless of the exigencies of our practical situations at least his advice should provide inspiration.

The key term *rikpa* or *rigpa* always requires annotation because we have yet to agree upon an English equivalent. 'Knowledge', 'intrinsic awareness', 'gnosis', 'total presence', and rikpa untranslated, have all been superseded in this translation by 'pure presence'. Rikpa could also be rendered as 'nondual awareness', and in rikpa's 'nondual' nature lies the problem because what is 'nondual' is beyond concept and expression. 'Emptiness in essence, clarity in nature, and compassion in expression' is as far as the tradition will go in denominating rikpa.

Homage to my Guru-Lama Dudjom Rinpoche, whose work and life provided a brilliant paradigmatic example of a Tibetan *rikzin*'s responsiveness. Immensely generous and skillful in means, he lived during an extremely difficult historical moment for his tradition. Further, through this short but seminal exposition of the Dzogchen view, Dudjom Rinpoche places himself amongst the great masters of the Tibetan language and yogis of the tradition along with Longchenpa and Jigmelingpa.

The first rendition into English of this difficult text was done by John Reynolds in 1978 as *Alchemy of Accomplishment*. The following year it was superseded by an excellent – if somewhat puritanical – translation called *Extracting the Quintessence of Accomplishment* done by Dudjom Rinpoche's literary mandala at Orgyen Kunsang Chokhorling in Darjeeling, Bengal, India. That work may be considered the 'authoritative' translation. But in this present translation, edited incrementally over the years, I have attempted to bring the translation one step closer to contemporary English usage while choosing English equivalents that reflect my personal appreciation of the author's intention.

The Tibetan title is *Ri chos bslab bya nyams len dmar khrid go bder brjod pa grub pa'i bcud len* and is published in Tibetan script in *Extracting the Quintessence of Accomplishment*.

Keith Dowman
Mt Abu, Rajasthan, India
1999

Homage to Kyabje Dudjom Rinpoche!

The author of this *Mountain Dharma* is one of the great masters of the Dzogchen dharma in these latter days. Among those who were aware of his life and work he was known to live in the stratosphere of Dzogchen achievement. That he was virtually unknown except to an inner circle of yogins and scholars is evidence of the invisibility that protected his family and his dharma, and the humility that enwrapped his precious life. His scholarship, made tangible in his books, is an external mark of his brilliance, but in the minds of those who knew him his personal radiance and kindness is a better index of his achievement. As a young and impressionable acolyte and pilgrim in the sixties, I knew him a little from afar, but I felt then as I still do fifty years later that I gained concord with one of the buddha-hearts of his generation.

In 1967 in Kalimpong, West Bengal, I met Dudjom Rinpoche for the first time. At our ringing of the bell, he himself opened the door of the rose-covered portico of his English-style cottage on the outskirts of Kalimpong in the foothills of the eastern Himalayas. We offered him a katak, fruit and the letter of introduction from Tulku Pema Wongyel, Kanjur Rinpoche's son, our friend and mentor. Rinpoche invited us in, sat us down and offered us tea and overwhelmed us with an avuncular display of generosity. He inquired after Kanjur Rinpoche, and he immediately understood that we were like Kanjur Rinpoche's children. He told us that he and Kanjur Rinpoche were one and the same, which in my mind seemed to conjure a Janus type two-headed guru-deity. Like a koan that induces experience of the nature of buddha-reality, this pronouncement was the first and most lasting of his verbal introductions to the nature of mind and was to stay with me until the now. Dudjom Rinpoche then took us to visit his Zangdok Peri gompa which was then in process of construction around the mountain in Kalimpong.

A few years later Dudjom Rinpoche came with his wife and daughters to live in Kathmandu, where we were then living, and we had more access to him. On certain days he was available for *darshan*, for blessing, for providing oracular answers to personal problems, or for answering scholarly enquiries or discussing meditation issues. On such an occasion in 1979 he blessed the rings that my wife, Meryl White, and I exchanged in a loose ceremony that did not bind us together as man and wife until death did us part but rather provided a sense of spiritual union in Dzogchen. Besides the elevated sense of Dzogchen that was always available in our meetings with him, there prevailed in us a sense of urgency to receive the atiyoga Dzogchen precepts from this most perfect tulku and lama. From time to time when the moment appeared propitious, we would prevail upon him for formal precepts. On one occasion, with my friend Mario Magglietti, we encountered him just as he prepared to leave the house and in a flurry of hurry took us with him along the lanes in the vicinity and out onto the main palace road, and as we three picked our way across that wide tightly crowded thoroughfare he gave us the discursive Dzogchen instruction on 'abiding, moving and pure presence' (*gnas 'gyu rig gsum*), one of the more mind (read *'intellect'*) boggling Dzogchen precepts, and then, when we reached the footpath on the other side of the road, he sent us away.

Dudjom Rinpoche was a family man, husband to a high society second wife, in the seventies parenting two attractive teenage daughters. His house was full of Kathmandu family life, in the middle of which Rinpoche appeared to sit with an imperturbable buddha smile. But in his ritual stance he carried the sense of higher seriousness to a level of perfect awareness. This stance was demonstrated optimally when in the winter of 1977-78 he gave the empowerments and permissions for the practice of the *Dudjom Tersar*, the canon of ritual and yogic texts that his tulku predecessor, Dudjom Lingpa, and he himself, had revealed. Just outside the built-up area of Boudha, off the main road, several paddy fields were covered in tented canvas and every day for a month, the Nyingma Dzogchen fraternity, tulkus and gomchens, the cream of Himalayan hermits, yogins, scholars and monks, together with droves of hardy lay people, coming from every nook and cranny of the Tibetan ethnic area, gathered to receive *wong* and *lung* (empowerment and authorization), together with blessings from the most vaunted lama in the Tibetan exodus. Some days were warm and dry and a smiling picnic vibe prevailed; sometimes it was cold and wet, and morose lay people piled in and fought for dry spaces. The privileged Injis sat, no less wet, in a secluded area – perhaps there were twenty of us there. Thus, Dudjom Rinpoche receiving his just and well-deserved acclamation in the mud of exile, transmitted the heart of his dharma.

In 1970 through pure happenstance, we were present in Delhi in the Ashoka Hotel when Sonam Kasi was paying his respects to Dudjom Rinpoche before his departure for the USA, where in New York he was to become an esteemed teacher of the Nyingma dharma. Harold Talbot, the erstwhile American secretary of an itinerant Christian monk, who was then a devoted acolyte of Dudjom Rinpoche (and later the editor of Tulku Thondrup's translations), was one of those present. At this gathering I first encountered Sogyal Rinpoche, the heart-son of Jamyang Khyentse Chokyi Lodro, one of the Tibetan Nyingma aristocracy and lama elite. Sogyal founded 'Rigpa', the Dzogchen sect, in London, which more than any other organization was to represent the Nyingma school in the UK. I am including Sogyal Rinpoche's eulogy of Dudjom Rinpoche here because while catching the extraordinary devotion that Dudjom Rinpoche inspired in those who received his blessing, it details his achievements in this world. These following paragraphs are taken from the foreword to *Dunjom Lingpa's Visions of the Great Perfection*:[1]

I would like to take this opportunity to share a few memories of Kyapjé Düdjom Rinpoché, whom I had the privilege and blessing of knowing personally. I first met him thanks to my master Jamyang Khyentsé Chökyi Lodrö. He always used to talk about what a wonderful and realized master Düdjom Rinpoché was, and how he was the living representative of Guru Padmasambhava.

---

[1] *The Vajra Essence: Dudjom Lingpa's Visions of the Great Perfection: Volume 3*, translated by B. Alan Wallace, Foreword by Sogyal Rinpoche, pp.xi-xv, (Wisdom Publications, Somerville, USA, 2015.)

Preface 17

They held each other in the highest esteem. In Lhasa, where they met in the 1950s, Düdjom Rinpoché confided to [the late] Trulshik Rinpoché that he considered Jamyang Khyentsé the holiest master they could ever hope to find. Düdjom Rinpoché moved to Kalimpong in India about 1957, and my master [Jamyang Khyentse] took me to meet him and receive blessings. Düdjom Rinpoché gave him the "seal of authorization" for all of his own terma treasures. He also conferred on Jamyang Khyentsé the empowerments and instructions for his mind treasure of Dorjé Drölo, the wild, wrathful aspect of Guru Padmasambhava. They wrote long-life prayers for each other. My master spoke of Düdjom Rinpoché as "the authentic great Sovereign Lord of the extraordinary and profound secret terma treasures." Düdjom Rinpoché called him "the sole champion in our time of the great and supreme path of the Vajra Heart Essence, the magical wisdom manifestation of the lotus-born lord Padmasambhava and Vimalamitra."

Some years later, I went to visit Düdjom Rinpoché in Kalimpong and by coincidence found myself translating for one of his American disciples. It was then that I realized just how extraordinary he was. By the end of his teaching, a pointing-out instruction of the nature of mind, tears were running down my face, and I understood what Jamyang Khyentsé had meant when he said this was an exceptional master. I instantly felt enormous faith in him, and there and then I requested Düdjom Rinpoché to be my master and grant me teachings.

Düdjom Lingpa's revelations and Düdjom Rinpoché's terma cycles are together known as the *Düdjom Tersar*, the "New Treasures of Düdjom," which are new in the sense that they are still fresh with the warm breath of the dakinis, and because there is only one master in the lineage between Guru Rinpoché and the practitioners of the heart treasures. Although I see these two great masters as one and the same, their outward characters were quite different. Düdjom Lingpa was a commanding and unpredictable figure, known for his wrathful demeanor and unpredictable behavior. Here Düdjom Rinpoché describes how to visualize him: "His body is red in color, his beard reaching as far as his heart, and his eyes are open wide, staring steadily straight ahead. His long hair is mostly tied up in a knot on top of his head with a small sacred book, while the rest tumbles loosely over his shoulders. He wears a gown of reddish brown silk, a shawl of white cotton, and conch-shell earrings, with a sword of wisdom thrust through his belt. His right hand wields a Vajra in the sky, and his left hand rolls a *purba* dagger of meteoric iron. He sits with his left leg stretched out slightly in the posture of royal play."

In marked contrast, Düdjom Rinpoché had about him an air of captivating kindness, gentleness, and serenity. In fact, he used to tell a story about his predecessor that always brought a twinkle to his eye. When Düdjom Lingpa was about to pass away and leave this world, some of his disciples approached him timidly and begged him to return in a more peaceful form. He chuckled and said, "Well, all right. But don´t complain if I am too peaceful."

Like his previous incarnation, Düdjom Rinpoché was a very great Dzokchen master. It is said of him that he was the body emanation of Khyeuchung Lotsawa, the speech emanation of Yeshé Tsogyal, and the mind emanation of

Guru Padmasambhava. In *The Tibetan Book of Living and Dying*, I tried to sum up some of his characteristics: "He was small, with a beautiful and gentle face, exquisite hands, and a delicate, almost feminine presence. He wore his hair long and tied up like a yogin in a knot; his eyes always glittered with secret amusement. His voice seemed the voice of compassion itself, soft and a little hoarse." One of the Padmasambhava´s terma prophecies captured his qualities with remarkable prescience: "In a noble family will appear an emanation of Khyeuchung Lotsawa bearing the name Jnana, keeping the yogic discipline of a master of mantras, his appearance not fixed in any way, his behavior spontaneous like a child, and endowed with piercing wisdom. He will reveal new termas and safe ward the ancient ones, and he will guide whoever has a connection with him to the Glorious Copper Colored Mountain in Ngayab Ling."

Düdjom Rinpoché, I learned, began receiving termas when he was a young boy, and he met Guru Rinpoché and Yeshé Tsogyal in a vision when he was only thirteen. Although he revealed his own powerful terma treasures, he decided to give priority to maintaining, protecting, and spreading the older termas as well as the Kama tradition of the Nyingmapas. While still quite young, he was regarded as a supreme master of the great perfection, and by the time he was in his thirties he had already accomplished an enormous amount. When other lamas saw his famous prayer *Calling the Lama from Afar*, which he composed at the age of thirty and which captured completely his profound realization, they immediately recognized his as a great tertón and Dzokchen master. Chökyi Nyima Rinpoché told me that his father, Tulku Urgyen Rinpoché, one of the greatest teachers of Dzokchen and Mahamudra in recent times, used to say that if anyone ever wondered what a true Dzokchen master and practitioner was like, they only had to look at Düdjom Rinpoché. His eyes always sparkled with a kind of freshness and vibrant clarity. Unencumbered by opinions of good and bad, and ever carefree, spacious, and relaxed, Düdjom Rinpoché had about him a child-like innocence – you could call it an enlightened purity.

His work in compiling the *Nyingma Kama,* which he began at the age of seventy-four, paralleled the achievement of Jamgön Kongtrul in compiling the treasure teaching in *The Precious Treasury of Termas* [*Rinchen gter mdzod*]. He saved many precious texts and sacred relics from loss, and with meticulous care, he compiled, preserved, emended, and annotated the older texts and practices, to the extent that there seems hardly anything he did not have a hand in perfecting. In fact, Düdjom Rinpoché´s achievements for the Nyingma tradition as a whole were monumental. He gave the transmission of the *Precious Treasury of Termas* ten times, and he transmitted the Kama [*Rnying ma bka' ma*] and the Hundred Thousand Tantras of the Nyingmapas [*Rnying ma rgyud 'bum*] as well as countless treasure cycles and priceless teaching. Unanimously requested to become the supreme head of the Nyingma tradition in exile, his own revelations and writings fill twenty-five volumes, among which his *History of the Nyingmapas* and *Fundamentals of the Nyingmapas* are classics. His compositions were amazing, his scholarship famous, his calligraphy much copied, his poetry lucid yet profound, and his detailed knowledge of every aspect of Vajrayana practice and ritual truly phenomenal.

Düdjom Rinpoché also played a huge part in reestablishing Tibetan culture and education in exile, and he composed his *History of Tibet* at the request of His Holiness the Dalai Lama. On occasion, His Holiness has expressed his regret at not having been able to receive transmissions directly from Düdjom Rinpoché, although when he embarked on a retreat on the Kabgyé – Eight Great Practice Mandalas – according to the *sangwa gyachen* pure visions of the great Fifth Dalai Lama, Düdjom Rinpoché wrote a practice guide for him that he found outstanding. Among Düdjom Rinpoché's countless disciples were the most eminent lamas of the last century, including the most senior masters of Mindröling and Dorjé Drak monasteries, and he had innumerable followers all over Tibet and the Himalayas, Europe, America, Taiwan, and Hong Kong. When he gave the transmission of the *New Treasures of Düdjom* at Bodhanath in Nepal in 1977-78, countless thousands upon thousands flocked to attend.

After my master Jamyang Khyentsé passed away, Düdjom Rinpoché held me with all his care and compassion, and I had the privilege of serving as his translator for a number of years. I quickly discovered that he had a unique way of inspiring the realization of the innermost nature of mind. It was through the very way he spoke. The words he used were simple and down to earth, and yet they had a way of penetrating right into your heart. As the instructions on the nature of mind flowed effortlessly from his wisdom mind, it seemed as if he became the teaching of Dzokpachenpo itself, and his words served to gather you into the actual experience. Through his presence, and through his gaze, he created a subtle but electrifying atmosphere, enveloping you in his wisdom mind, so that you could not help but feel the pure awareness that he was pointing at. I can only compare it to sitting in front of a blazing, open fire –you cannot help but feel warm. It was as simple as that. Düdjom Rinpoché demonstrated, again and again, that when a great master directs the blessing of his wisdom mind, something extraordinary and very powerful can take place. All your ordinary thoughts and thinking are disarmed, and you arrive face to face with the deeper nature – the original face – of your own mind. In Düdjom Rinpoche's words, "all the stirrings of discursive thoughts melt, dissolve, and slip into the expanse of rikpa, your pure awareness, which is like a cloudless sky. All their power and strength is lost to the rikpa awareness." At the moment everything drops, a completely different dimension opens up, and you glimpse the sky-like nature of mind. With Düdjom Rinpoché I came to understand that what the master does, through the power and blessing of his realization, is to make the naked truth of the teaching come alive in you, connecting you to your Buddha nature. And you? You recognize, in a blaze of gratitude, that there is not, and could never be, any separation between the master´s wisdom mind and the nature of your own mind. Düdjom Rinpoché said just this in *Calling the Lama from Afar:*

Since pure awareness of nowness is the real Buddha,
In openness and contentment I found the lama in my heart.
When we realize this unending natural mind is the very
      nature of the lama,
Then there is no need for attached, grasping, or weeping
      prayers or artificial complaints.
By simply relaxing in this uncontrived, open,
      and natural state,
We obtain the blessing of aimless self-liberation
      of whatever arises.

At the same time, Düdjom Rinpoché wore his realization and learning with such simplicity and ease. I sometimes felt that his outward appearance was so subtle and understated that it would have been easy for a newcomer to miss who he really was. Once in 1976 I traveled with him from France to the United States. I shall never forget that flight for as long as I live. Düdjom Rinpoché was always very humble, but now and then he would say something that betrayed what an incredible master he was. At one point I was sitting next to him and he was gazing out the window at the Atlantic Ocean when he said quietly, "May I bless all those I fly over, all the beings living in the ocean down below." I could feel that there was simply no question: He actually did possess the power to bless and relieve the suffering of countless living beings. And beyond any shadow of doubt, there and then, they were receiving his blessings. In that moment I realized what a great master he was – and not just a master, but a Buddha.

To tell the truth, even now, thirty years or so, since he left this world, Düdjom Rinpoché's greatness still continues to dawn on me, day after day. The gratitude I feel toward him is boundless, and not a day goes by when I do not think of his words:

Purifying karmic delusion, the heart´s darkness,
The sun's radiant light continuously arises;
Such fortune is the lamas' inexpressible kindness:
Lama of unrepayable kindness, I remember only you!

Mountain Dharma

I bow down with devotion and take refuge at the feet of my glorious Guru-Lama, incomparable in grace. I pray that through his blessing I and my disciples may quickly reach the immaculate realization of the profound path in the nature of our minds and attain the existential citadel of the now in this very lifetime.

For those fortunate individuals whose deep aspirations and pure karmic propensities have now coincided and who have faith in the profound Dzogchen teaching and in the teacher who reveals it, this simple gateway explanation now in your hand is the quintessence of practice of the most sacred, mystical Dzogchen, being instruction on the main points of mountain retreat.

Apprehend this teaching by means of three main topics: The first topic is preparation – how to purify the mindstream by cutting clinging attachment and focusing the mind on the praxis. The second topic is the main endeavor – how to engage in the experiential praxis after eradicating misconceptions and doubts about view, meditation and action. The third topic is a stream of illuminated existential attainment – how to sustain the samayas and keep the vows and thus completely assimilate the karma of this lifetime to Dzogchen realization.

The First Topic: Preparation

First, a little about the first topic – preparation.

Oh, the mind, the mind has mountains, but this desolate mind with its scintillating highs and depressing troughs originates in the here and now with Kuntuzangpo, and Kuntuzangpo, knowing everything as himself, is absolutely free. Those who fail to recognize mind's nature, however, are flung around on the endlessly spinning wheel of life. Through time, they experience innumerable permutations of the six bodymind syndromes, where their lives have no meaning, the syndromes of human beings, gods, titans, hungry ghosts, animals and hell beings.

Now that you have attained this outside chance of a human birth, you must use it to avoid rebirth in the lower realms. If you fail in this, you cannot know where you will be reborn after death, and no matter which of the six states is your destiny suffering will afflict you. Further, to attain a human body is not enough – the moment of your death is uncertain and you must act appropriately in that very moment. If you do the right thing now, at the moment of death, you, like Milarepa, will feel no shame or regret. Said Milarepa at the moment of his death, "My inner life gives me no cause for any self reproach".

Entering upon this spiritual quest, you should adopt outer, conventional, appearances. But more important than that, here and now, you must cut all attachment to the desirable qualities of fashion and show, and the mundane imperatives of existence. If the mind is not completely turned around and you once enter the gate of commitment with a loose compromising mind, residual attachment to homeland, wealth and property, family and friends, and so on, will follow you. In such a situation, the propensity for attachment as the primary cause and objects of attachment as circumstantial conditions will coincide to create pernicious obstacles. Then, again involved with the ordinary mundane world, you will backslide and regress.

So you should do what you can to deflate the importance of food, clothes, social interaction, and so on, and detaching yourselves from the eight mundane obsessions – loss and gain, pleasure and pain, anonymity and fame, praise and blame – you should direct the mind one-pointedly to the inner objective.

You must follow the example of Gyelwa Yangonpa, who said,

In the solitary place called Knowledge of Death
the hermit Disgusted With Attachment,
by abandoning all concern for this life,
draws the protecting mystic circle
and thus excludes the spirit-visitors'
eight mundane obsessions.

If you have not achieved such detachment, your inner life will be corrupted by those obsessions, which are as poisonous as tainted food.

The eight mundane obsessions may be reduced to hope and fear, which arise from attachment and aversion. Internal attachment and aversion take on the outer appearance of the demons *gyelpo* and *senmo* and so long as we are bound by attachment and aversion we are plagued by them and obstacles will not cease to arise.

Are there any residual conceits – temporal and mundane obsessions – lurking in the pit of your mind? Examine yourself constantly and focus on exterminating them. Harboring such ambitions while making the pretence of a spiritual life in order to make a living is gross hypocrisy and wrong livelihood.

"Abandoning your homeland is half of the quest!" is an ancient axiom. Put your home behind you and take to the road in unknown countries. Take cordial leave of your family and friends but ignore their attempts to dissuade you from your purpose. Give away your possessions and depend on whatever you receive as alms. Regard the desirable things of this life as stubborn obstacles produced by bad habits and cultivate a renunciate mindset. If in your attitude to possessions you fail to understand that a little is enough, when dissatisfaction with what you have arises it is easy for the consumerist demon to slip in.

Whatever people might say about you, good or bad, refraining from denial or affirmation, without attaching hopes or fears to it, don't believe it. Cultivate disinterest. Let them say whatever they like, as if they were talking about someone dead and buried.

Only real teachers – and that excludes both your parents – can tell us what to do. So keep your independence and don't let anyone lead you by the nose.

You should always be well disposed and good-natured and know how to relate harmoniously with people without putting anyone's nose out of joint. But when it comes down to the nitty-gritty and someone – no matter who it is – tries to disturb our sadhana, be intractable, immovable, like an iron boulder tugged at with a silk scarf. Don't be too easily moved and pliable; don't bend where the wind blows like grass on a mountain pass.

Whatever your sadhana may be, after vowing to complete it sustains it at any cost, even though your life be at risk – though thunderbolts fall from the heavens, floods issue from the earth below, and landslides rain around you, persevere to the end. To that purpose, from the start, gradually establish a strict schedule of meditation periods, meals, breaks and sleep, precluding bad habits creeping in. Your practice may be elaborate ritual or formless meditation, but don't leave it undisciplined so that you have time to waste; rather, pace yourself evenly.

When going into retreat, the hermitage door should be sealed with mud. Failing that, don't relate to anyone, don't speak to anyone, and don't spy.

Spurning the wanderings of the restless mind, expel stale breath, and assuming a good body posture let the mind relax into an all-pervasive presence without so much as a snap of distraction – be like a tent peg in frozen ground. A strict retreat in those outer, inner and secret dimensions will quickly produce the signs and qualities that are evidence of attainment.

If something of importance comes up and you weaken and relent and you meet someone and even talk with him, thinking, "After this I shall be more strict!" you will lose the dynamic of the retreat and become looser and looser. On the other hand, if you resolve right from the beginning to keep your seat and make no exceptions, your retreat will become increasingly disciplined and your sadhana will be free from any plague of obstacles.

There are many different recommendations to guide you to your actual place of retreat, but in general it should be somewhere that has been blessed by a master such as Guru Rinpoche. It should not be a place in the hands of people whose beliefs are antagonistic to your own. It should be an utterly solitary place where you feel completely at ease and where practicalities are not a problem. If you possess the capacity and strength to spontaneously resolve outer appearances and inner susceptibilities in cremation grounds, cemeteries and other wild places of negative energy where malignant spirits and demons abide, your meditation will be greatly inspired and swiftly fulfilled; if you lack such a capacity then all sorts of obstacles will arise in that kind of place. When realization is identical to the here and now all difficult situations appear as positive reinforce-ment and it is most beneficial at that time to do secret yogas in places like cremation grounds and graveyards. The real solitary place, though, is the space of nonaction after our mind-flow has become free of all self-indulgent inner and outer games.

As to the actual process of purification, this consists of the ordinary training in the four mind changes and the extraordinary training in refuge, aspiration, confession, and offering-meditation according to the oral instruction – persevere in this until the benefits are palpable. Thereafter make guru-yoga the mainstay of the training and work with that. Without these foundation practices meditation will be sluggish and even as it deepens it will be fraught with obstacles.

Until pure realization is the pervasive element in our being, pray with fervent heartfelt devotion and soon, through the transference of the heart-mind realization of the Lama, a wonderful inexpressible realization will spontaneously erupt within. Lama Shang Rinpoche said, "To find peace, to have mystic experience, to attain profound absorption, and so on, these are common experiences. Much more precious than that is realization, the realization born from within through the blessings of the Lama, the realization that arises out of fervent devotion."

The reality of Dzogchen suffusing the mind is directly dependant upon the preparation. That is why Je Drigung said, "Some traditions emphasize the main endeavor; our tradition stresses the preliminaries."

The Second Topic:
The Main Endeavor:
How to Engage Directly in the Practice after Eradicating Misconceptions and Doubts about View, Meditation and Action

Firstly, concerning the view that comprehends what really is, the ultimate nature of mind itself, its natural state of being free of all kinds of distinction that the differentiating mind imposes, is conventionally called *rikpa*, pure presence. Rikpa arises naked in the nondual awareness of the spontaneously manifest here and now. It is inexpressible in words and cannot be indicated by metaphor. It is not samsara's confusion nor nirvana's resolution. It is not born and it is not extinguished. It cannot be liberated and it cannot fall into error. It neither exists nor is it nonexistent. It is not infinite nor is it bounded in any direction.

In short, in the here and now, since it is not established as any specific thing, state or action, it has the original face of emptiness, pure from the beginning, which is all pervasive and all penetrating. Because the unobstructed lustre of emptiness and the innumerable constituents of samsara and nirvana are inseparable like the sun and its rays, emptiness is experienced positively as anything whatsoever and it has the intrinsic nature of nondual awareness of the spontaneously arisen universe of pure quality. So, the recognition of the presence of what is, as the natural state of being in the now, the 'real self' consisting of the three buddha bodies, pure presence as the union of light and emptiness, is called the view of the inconceivable Great Perfection

As the great master Padmasambhava said, "The inconceivable dharmakaya is the real nature of mind." Oh! what an inexpressible joy to hold Kuntuzangpo's mind in the palm of your hand!

This view is the quintessence of the sixty four hundred thousand tantras of the Great Perfection, which in turn are the essence of the eighty four thousand aspects of buddha teaching. There is nowhere to go beyond this and in this perspective you should resolve all your doubts, finally, on every level.

Secondly, now that all doubts and misconceptions regarding the Dzogchen view have been resolved, maintaining the continuity of that view is meditation. Forget all other kinds of meditation, mentally conceived and contrived meditations that have an object or some objective – you do nothing of that kind. Under the dispensation of the view elucidated above, its strength sustained, stay loose and relaxed in the natural flow of all the cognitions at the five sense doors.

To meditate with a collateral mental commentary identifying specific aspects of a process is not meditation. It is intellectual activity. In actuality, there is nothing whatsoever to meditate upon; and there is no process of meditation. But do not suffer a moment of inattention. To wander from self-awareness is real delusion, so don't be distracted! Whatever thoughts arise, let them arise, but don't follow them and don't block them.

What, then, is to be done? Whatever objective sensory information arises, as mere appearance the form is not to be clung to, but, rather, the pristine freshness of the experience is dwelt upon, just like a child's gaze moving around a magical temple without lodging anywhere. All momentary mental phenomena stays in its own place, its form undistorted, its colors unchanged, and its lustre constant. Further, by keeping sensory impressions unadulterated by desirous and grasping thoughts, all the visionary appearances of mind arise as the naked nondual awareness of luminous emptiness.

Some people of lesser intellectual training or capacity may be confused by all these "deep and spacious" teachings and if I were to condense the meaning of them all into one seminal indication for them, I would say this: In the gap between the cessation of one thought and the inception of the next, isn't there an immutable moment of here-and-now consciousness that is clear naked awareness? Ho! That is surely pure presence itself! And since you cannot stay in that space of pure suchness, doesn't a thought inevitably arise? That thought is the creative expression of pure presence! When you fail to recognize the thought in itself immediately it arises, it proliferates into wandering judgmental thought that could be called "a chain of delusion" and that is the origin of samsara. When you recognize the thought upon its inception and just let it be without running after it, whatever thought arises is spontaneously liberated into the space of pure presence, the dharmakaya.

In that meditation the strands of trekcho view and meditation are wound together. It constitutes the foundation of Dzogchen meditation. The adiguru, Garab Dorje said,

*The instantaneous recollection of pure presence
upon its sudden emergence
from the nature of the pure space in the now
is like finding a jewel at the bottom of the ocean:
this is the dharmakaya, uncontrived, made by no one.*

Abiding in this experience undistracted, both night and day, emptiness being an experiential reality, pure presence is our home.

Thirdly, through action, meditation is potentiated and practice is engaged directly.

I've said it before and I'll say it again, "Make no distinction even for an instant between the Guru-Lama and the Buddha himself, and pray to him from the heart with fervent devotion." Such devotion is the universal panacea and there is no better way to dispel obstacles, to potentiate your meditation, and to arrive directly at your destination.

About faults in meditation: When there is sinking and dullness, you need to arouse alert awareness; and when there is distraction and restlessness you must relax the mind deep within. Yet this cannot be done forcibly, by application of the flow of the flickering meditating mind, but, rather, simply by remembering to recognize the nature of mind. This recognition is sustained continuously, in all circumstances, while eating, sleeping, walking, sitting, and in every possible activity, in both formal meditation sessions and also in the intervals between them. Whatever thoughts arise, happy or sad, or in any way emotionally tainted, all thoughts are let alone without hope or fear, without rejecting them or cherishing them, and without any attempt to neutralize them with antidotes. Whatsoever feelings of joy or pain there may be, they are left in their true nature – undefiled, pristine, fresh and vivid. You will see that you always come back to the one main point, so don't worry your head with all kinds of psychological theories. Also, remember that it isn't necessary to focus on the emptiness aspect as an antidote to undesirable judg-mental thoughts and emotions. Simultaneous with their identification as pure presence they are reflexively liberated like a snake uncurling its knots.

These days all kinds of people know how to express verbally the ultimate hidden meaning of the Clear Light Vajra Heart (Wosel Dorje Nyingpo), but if they have no existential experience of it their litany is like a parrot's prattle. We are so very greatly fortunate!

Now there is something else you must understand. The two deadly enemies that have bound us to samsara from beginningless time are the Grasper and the Grasped. By the grace of the Guru-Lama's introduction to the self-abiding dharmakaya, those two enemies have now been consumed like a feather touched by flame, leaving no trace or residue. Isn't that a hit! But if you don't actualize the profound instruction of the direct method thus obtained, it is like placing a wish-fulfilling gem into the mouth of a corpse. What a waste! Don't let the mind rot away! Do it now!

About beginners' mind: You will find that black thoughts invade and suffuse the mind and inevitably and unavoidably create serious distraction. Such negative thought-trains will proliferate, leading you into unmindfulness where you will remain until a lucid recollection returns you to the light with the remorseful thought, "I have been wandering!" When this happens, don't interrupt such thoughts and don't feel guilty and so on, but just sustain the flow begun by the vivid regained recollection of the nature of mind.

"Do not reject your thoughts – see them as the dharmakaya." This oft quoted admonition is all very well, but until your capacity for heightened penetrating insight is realized, so long as you remain in a state of blank tranquillity, merely thinking, "this is the dharmakaya" leads to an uninspired equanimity in which there is no awareness of how things are in themselves, as such. So at the beginning simply stare non-discursively at thoughts as they arise, identifying with the knower (the recognizer) of the thoughts, like an old man watching children at play, looking without seeing, seeing without judging. Settled into this fixed gaze you will fall into a dead stream of thoughtlessness that will be suddenly destroyed [by the syllable PHAT, for example] and in that instant a mind transcending non-dual awareness will arise in all its naked clarity.

In the course of time, inevitably you will experience some bliss, clarity and thoughtlessness and if you remain free of all self-satisfaction, conceited attachment, hopes, and fears, you will not go astray.

It is of vital importance to abandon attachment to distractions and to meditate with single pointed attention. Falling into intellectual analysis in intermittent meditation experience, tranquil concentration will be overwhelmed and you will be vain and complacent. Failing to penetrate the seductive aspects of deep meditative experience, gaining mere facility in verbal and poetic expression, no benefit will accrue.

Remember the old Dzogchen adages "Intellectual understanding is like a patch – it wears out," and "Mystical or psychedelic experience is like mist – it fades away." Even adepts can be deceived by trivial circumstances – good or bad – and get lost in them. And even after the impact of meditation has hit the mind, unless it is cultivated continuously the profound precepts will remain only on the pages of the book. Real meditation cannot come out of an untamed mind, a wild approach or an undisciplined practice. You hoary meditators, still novices in practice, look out! You may die with salt encrusted minds!

After you have accustomed yourself to this mode over a long period, due to devotion or some such factor, existential experience will become realization and you will see pure presence naked and shining. Like taking a longtime hood off your head, it's such a relief! – blindness is replaced by supreme vision. Wandering thought now arises as meditation, and quiescence and movement are liberated alike. At first, recognition of thoughts is like meeting an old friend. Later, the reflexive liberation of thoughts is like a snake untying its knots. Finally, the unaffective liberation of thoughts is like a thief standing in an empty house. You will experience these three modes of release progressively. A strong, immutable conviction will arise from within that all phenomena are a magical display of pure presence. Billows of emptiness and compassion will burst forth. The tendency to distinguish between samsara and nirvana dissolves. No moral distinction is made between buddha and sentient beings. No matter what you do you cannot be shaken out of the space of the comfortable reality of mind's nature in a twenty-four hour a day continuum. So it is said in Dzogchen: "Realization, like the sky, is unchangeable."

The yogi with this realization has the body of an ordinary person, but his mind abides in the buddha dynamic of effortless dharmakaya and he traverses in nonaction all the paths and stages.

At the end, intellect exhausted, purpose extinguished, like the interior space of a broken bottle united with exterior space, the body dissolves into atoms and the mind dissolves into the nature of reality. This is called "transmutation into the vase body of youth", the inner radiance of the primordial ground continuum. And so it shall be. This culmination of view, meditation and action is called the actualization of the unattainable goal. The seemingly integral levels of existential experience and realization can arise progressively, in no particular order, or instantaneously, according to the capacity of the individual. But at the time of consummation and culmination, no distinctions exist.

The Third Topic:
The Stream of Illuminated Existential Attainment: How to Sustain the Samayas and Keep the Vows and Completely Assimilate the Karma of this Lifetime to Dzogchen Realization.

If you sustain the practice of Dzogchen view, meditation and action but lack some facility in skillful means in daily life, during activity on the path, during the gaps in formal meditation, inevitably your samaya commitments and vows will be broken. In this case your progress will be interrupted, obstacles will arise, and it is certain that eventually you will fall into the avichi hell. It is vital, therefore, that you never leave the corral of mindfulness and recollection of mind's nature maintaining perfect discrimination. The great master Padmasambhava said, "My view is as high as the sky, but my reflexive analysis of cause and effect is finer than dust." So, avoiding impulsiveness, you must be highly sensitive to the laws of karma. Keep your commitments and maintain even the slightest promise unbroken and you will avoid the ignominy of moral fault and downfall.

All the many and various tantric samayas can be subsumed under the samayas of the Guru-Lama's body, speech and mind. "When you conceive of the Guru-Lama as an ordinary man for even a split second, realization is still light years away." Why is this? "The disciple's realization is contingent upon the Master."

That is the crucial point. Whoever you are, so long as you have no Guru you are reliant upon your fallible self. After taking a Guru-Lama, the bonds of initiation and oral instruction give you no choice but to keep the samayas. After you have taken the four initiations, bow before the Guru-Lama, the principal of the mandala, and say, "From now on I offer myself to you as a servant. Accept me as your disciple and use every part of me." However high or mighty you may be, aren't you binding yourself to the Guru-Lama by this declaration? You should add, "Whatever the Guru asks, so I will do." After making this promise, can you deny him anything? And if you don't fulfil your promise, aren't you a liar, however unpleasant that may sound?

It has never been said that you should keep your commitment to the great lamas inviolate, lamas who have many followers and who are rich and powerful and generous, while you can ignore your commitment to lesser, humble, lamas, who hold mean positions like beggar ascetics. Whatever type of lama you have, you must understand the pros and cons of the samaya, and not sit bewildered like an old lame workhorse. Is the imperative to keep the samaya for the lama's benefit or your own? Think it over carefully, long and deep. If it's for the lama's benefit, you can forget it right now; but if it's for your own sake, don't cut your own throat.

The general commitment to your buddhist brothers and sisters is to hold everyone who enters the door of buddha's teaching in high esteem, cultivating a pure vision. Forsake all philosophical sectarianism, prejudice and bias. The specific commitment to the community of vajra-brothers and sisters united by a single Guru-Lama in a single mandala is avoidance of all contempt, rivalry, jealousy and deceit, and always to treat the entire community as intimate friends.

"All sentient beings at some time or another have been my loving parents and now they are afflicted by fierce suffering on the unstoppable wheel of life. If I do not help them, who else will?" Motivated by this thought, train your mind in contemplation of compassion. If you can accomplish some benefit by thought, word or deed dedicate all the merit to others. Always thinking only about the path, the lama and sentient beings, don't let your deeds conflict with your intentions. When tempted to compete with those who possess the name and signs of monks or yogis, swallow your words and control yourselves. This is extremely important. Don't make a fool of yourself by arguing, no matter what the so-called "truth" is, regardless of right or wrong.

If you come to think about the possibility of your own enlightenment only in a future life, remember that what is required must be done by yourself before the moment of death. If you put your faith in death rites conducted by others as a source of merit for yourself, you may be disappointed. So summon the mind back inside, and filled with disgust for worldly concerns lay the foundation with a strong resolution to remember that life and sadhana are one. Then in the practice of view and meditation incisively hit the target of the main endeavor. In the subsequent illuminated stream of existence the method of maintaining the samayas, keeping your vows and applying your instructions, is to avoid what is destructive and adopt what is beneficial. Your quality-potential will then involuntarily be ful-filled. That is why Dzogchen is such a powerful tool for sinners on the way to buddha.

Obstacles arise on this path due to its great profundity – although advantage is commensurate with risk. All the karmic negativity accumulated in many past lives is potentiated by the Guru-Lama's precepts and manifests externally as fiendish paranoid illusions, the tricks of maras. At your power-place retreat, gods and demons may show their forms and call you by name. They may appear as your Guru to give false prophetic injunctions. Various paranoid illusions may arise in vision or dream. In the common light of day, you may actually be subjected to beating, cutting, abuse, shit, theft, disease and other unpredictable afflictions. You may suffer severe anxiety attacks without any apparent reason. You may shake and weep uncontrollably. Intense passionate emotions can dominate. You may lose your devotion, aspiration and compassion. Paranoid thoughts arise and drive you out of your mind. You misunderstand kind words. You bitterly resent the retreat you have imposed upon yourself and wish to escape and abandon your good intentions. You project mean ideas upon the Guru. Insidious doubts arise about your path. You may find yourself falsely accused; acquire a bad reputation, while close friends turn against you. All sorts of unwanted internal and external situations may occur. These situations are existential crises. Recognize them as such. They provide decisive moments. If you deal with them incisively they become a source of power and realization. If you fall under their sway they become demonic obstructions.

In the latter case, with pure samaya and persistent unwavering devotion, entrust your mind and heart to the Guru-Lama and pray fervently to him knowing that he is omniscient. Take these adverse situations as eminently desirable, and bringing fierce application to the practice, sooner or later the potent forces of adverse situation will surely collapse into themselves and your practice will become inspired. Appearances will seem like mist. You will gain strong confidence in the Guru-Lama's instructions. And next time such crises arise, you will greet them with fond assurance. That is the point of resolution. Assimilating difficult situations to the path, crises are resolved. Wonderful! That's what we old men like to see! Don't be like a jackal stalking a human corpse with trembling haunches! Be of strong mind!

Then there are those individuals whose pile of merit is small, whose samaya and vows are lax, whose inverted views are unrelenting, whose doubts are many, and whose promises are high but practice feeble. Such people – with hearts like acrid flatulence – entreat the Guru's precepts to stay on top of the bookshelf. In the event of adverse circumstances they will take the hand of death, following the path of least resistance, and mara seizing the opportunity will lead them down the slope to the lower realms. Shame on them! Pray to the Guru that that does not happen to you!

Adverse situations arising on the path may be easily dealt with, while positive situations present far greater difficulties. If you are still conceited about your high realization, you are in danger of fixating on this life's great opportunities alone, and becoming a slave to the fiendish temptations of divine pleasure and power. You must be very careful! You must understand that at such a juncture, where the great meditator is weighed in the balance, you can go up or down.

Until the expression of the qualities of your inner realization is fully potentiated, don't recount your mystical experiences, however significant, to anyone. Keep your mouth shut. And don't boast about your months or years in retreat. Rather, apply yourself to meditation practice for the duration of your life. Under the influence of an intellect intoxicated by mere talk of emptiness, don't despise conventionally motivated moral behavior. Don't stay long in towns where shaman rites of demon subjection and such are being performed just to fill your stomach. Minimize meaningless activity, unnecessary talk, and useless cogitation. Don't try to turn people's heads by priestcraft or cleverness contrary to the teaching. Don't engage in wrong livelihood by means of devious or flattering speech motivated by longing for desirable things. Don't hang out with people with irreconcilable view or lifestyle. Don't associate with wicked people. Gratuitously reveal your own faults but don't disclose the hidden faults of others.

It is said that all kinds of tobacco are the tools of disease-spreading demons, so seriously give it up. Alcohol is an element of the samaya, but don't imbibe with abandon to the point of intoxication.

Gather on the path all kinds of people, making no distinction between those with whom you have good and bad relationship, including both honest people who may give you respect and dishonest people who may hate you and slander you.

Always, sustaining an inward exalted high, with courageous, undaunted awareness, take a lowly social place and follow a humble course of action. Wear second hand clothes, for example. Place everyone – good, bad or indifferent – above your self. Live an alternative lifestyle and stay in hermitages as much as you can. Make the beggar your ideal. Take the old masters' existential modes and lifestyles as the highest example. Don't blame your karma, but keep your path pure; and don't complain about present circumstances, but whatever happens use it to advantage.

In short, make your own mind the witness and integrate this teaching into your life, so that at the time of death, with your mind free of mere good intentions, you will be without self-reproach. There lies the point of all your practice. When the time of your death arrives, you will be able to leave all your wealth and possessions without the least attachment to even a button. At the moment of death, the superior yogi will be ecstatic, the middling yogi will be fearless, and the ordinary yogi will feel no regret. In whosoever the clear light of realization shines night and day throughout the universe, there will be no bardo and the body will just dissolve. If that does not occur, then liberated in the bardo with a crystal clear mind all things shall be well. If that does not happen, when the time is ripe, apply the practice of sublimation in which you have previously trained and in which you have gained some experience, and after transferring to the buddhafield of your preference you will traverse the remaining paths and stages and attain buddha.

In our precious tradition, the realization of buddha is not some pie-in-the-sky legend. Even nowadays through the culminating realization on the paths of trekcho and togal, corporeality is transformed into a rainbow body, a pile of light. So don't throw away this precious jewel in exchange for some glass trinket. You are extremely fortunate to have found the dakini's lifeblood here in the form of these profound instructions. Calling your pure mind to witness, therefore, rejoice and meditate! You who follow me should regard this book as a heart treasure and great benefit will ensue.

Colophon

The purpose of this teaching was support of the retreat practice of the meditators of The Island of the Highest Lotus Light (Ogmin Padma Woling). It was facilitated by the request of Rikzang Dorje who possessed the gem of immutable faith and devotion. It was spoken from the heart as quintessential personal advice by Jigtral Yeshe Dorje (Dudjom Rinpoche). May awareness of the nondual arise ineradicably in the minds of all fortunate beings.

Glossary of Technical Terms

bardo:	intermediate state
dharmakaya:	nondual existential mode
mara:	personification of obstacle arising in meditation
sadhana:	spiritual praxis
samaya	commitment, vow,
tantra	scripture of Vajrayana
togal	'leapover' phase of Dzogchen realization
trekcho	'breakthrough' phase of Dzogchen realization
tulku	buddha-emanation embodiment
vajra	ritual instrument; adamantine
Vajrayana	Sacred Word approach to buddha, tantrayana
yoga	recognition of union

Other Titles by Keith Dowman

Everything is Light: *A Great Explanatory Dzogchen Tantra, The Circle of Total Illumination.* A Dzogchen Now! Book.

Guru Pema Here and Now: The Mythology of the Lotus-Born, A Dzogchen Now! Book

The Yeshe Lama. Jigme Lingpa's Dzogchen Manual, A Dzogchen Now! Book

Spaciousness: The Radical Dzogchen of the Vajra-Heart (Longchenpa), A Dzogchen Now! Book

Original Perfection: Vairotsana's Five Early Transmissions, Wisdom Publications. Also, *The Eye of the Storm*, Vajra Books

The Great Secret of Mind: Instruction on Nonduality in Dzogchen (Tulku Pema Riktsal), Shambhala.

Maya Yoga: Finding Comfort and Ease in Enchantment (Longchenpa), A Dzogchen Now! Book

Natural Perfection (Longchenpa), Wisdom Publications. Also, *Old Man Basking in the Sun*, Vajra Books.

The Flight of the Garuda (Shabkar Rinpoche) Wisdom Publications

The Sacred Life of Tibet (HarperCollins)

Power-Places of Kathmandu, Inner Traditions

Boudhanath: The Great Stupa

Masters of Enchantment, Inner Traditions

The Power-Places of Central Tibet: The Pilgrims Guide, RKP, Pilgrims, Vajra Books

Masters of Mahamudra, SUNY

Sky Dancer: The Secret Life and Songs of the Lady Yeshe Tsogyal, Penguin, Shambhala

The Nyingma Icons, Dzogchen Now! Books

The Divine Madman: The Life and Songs of Drukpa Kunley, Dzogchen Now! Books

The Legend of the Great Stupa, Dharma Publishing

Calm and Clear: A Manual of Buddhist Meditation, Dharma Publishing

See www.keithdowman.net and www.radicaldzogchen.com for details of publications and the public talks of Keith Dowman.

2017

Printed in Great Britain
by Amazon